Haiku
STAT!

A Poetic Look at the Harsh Realities
of Emergency Medicine.

Jason Hautala

ISBN: 1463650426
ISBN-13: 9781463650421
Library of Congress Control Number:
2011911144

In memory of
My friend, Jaesun Frank Hora.
Hero to many.

Disclaimer

The views expressed in this book are *not* the views of any hospital, agency, or facility in which I have volunteered or worked. If it will save me from getting fired, let me state that some of the views may not even be my own.

This book is not intended to diagnose, treat, cure, or prevent any disease or medical condition. Ask your primary care doctor, or better yet, check yourself into the nearest emergency department if you have any questions.

Table of Contents

Acknowledgments

Thank you to my family, friends, and co-workers who encouraged me to pursue this project. I would have never accomplished this without your support. Thank you also for your help with editing the manuscript, but most importantly, thank you for putting up with someone like me. It is not everyone who can appreciate a friend who can watch someone die and then say, "Hey! That would make a good haiku."

Introduction

Haiku is a traditional style of poetry from Japan that typically follows a rhythm of 5-7-5 sound units. Sound units and syllables are not the same, but the English version of Haiku follows a rhythm of 5-7-5 syllables. Haiku were made to describe aspects of the various seasons.

This book breaks several rules of the traditional Haiku, but it does give an insightful look into the life and struggles in the emergency department.

This project started when my hospital put out notice that if employees wanted to display any of their artwork or write an article for the next hospital newsletter, they had until a certain date to submit. The first ten haiku of this book are the first ten that I wrote and submitted for publication. The rejection letter went something like this: "While I laughed at some of them, they will not be getting published." Like most ER folks, I enjoy a good challenge, so I wrote 200 more and published them myself.

The scenes described in this book are all true. They come from my time spent as an EMS volunteer, student, hospital employee, and an officer with a combat support hospital in the Army Reserves. My current employer has opted out of being officially recognized in this book, so let me say that the Emergency Department at Man's Greatest Hospital is a wonderful place to work, but even here, the stresses of the job can make some people break down and start writing poetry.

I hope you enjoy reading these as much as I have enjoyed writing them. For the non-medical folks that have picked up a copy of this book, underlined words may be found in the glossary of terms. The glossary is not intended to provide dictionary definitions, but rather, a more realistic understanding of the terms. It has also been moved from the end of the book to the pre-Haiku section so that everyone will have a chance to enjoy the definitions.

Glossary of Terms

AMA: Against Medical Advice. No matter how stupid the choices patients make, they still have the right to do so. It is polite to caution them not to let the door hit them on the ass on the way out.

APS: Adult Protective Services is similar to CPS (Child Protective Services) but for old people. Not sure which call makes me madder. Some family members just need to be shot.

Aberrancy: Wide complex on the EKG showing slowed electrical transmission. Can be confused with ventricular rhythms. It is also a term my psychiatrist used when describing my poetry.

Accreditation: A process of showing the paper pushers of the world that we are doing everything "right." No matter what the *working* policies are, the *written* policies and the procedures performed while under observation of the accrediting body will be right, no matter how wrong and inefficient they are.

Activated charcoal: Liquefied BBQ briquettes. Used to bind to chemicals that have been ingested, to prevent them from being absorbed into the blood. Very messy stuff. Just from reading about it, you had better call housekeeping.

Adenosine: Medicine that stops the heart for a few seconds with the hope that it will have a better rhythm when it starts back up again. Those few seconds of flatline can seem like a long time to both the patient and the staff.

Alpha-1 antitrypsin: Used by the body to control the restructuring of lung tissue. Smoking destroys it, so your body breaks down lung tissue faster than it builds it.

Ammonia snap: Ammonia inhalant. Glass vial that releases ammonia gas when broken. Used to convince people that pretending to be unconscious or having a seizure just isn't worth it.

"Another One Bites the Dust": An excellent song by Queen that not only has realistic lyrics, but is at the correct tempo for proper CPR.

Atropine: Medicine derived from deadly nightshade. It is used in large amounts for organophosphate toxicity.

Avascular necrosis: The dying of tissue, such as bone, due to lack of blood supply.

BM: Bowel Movement: Medical term for going poop, pinching a loaf, dropping a deuce, etc.

Banana bag: Normal saline IV with multivitamins, thiamine, and folate added to it. Mostly used on alcoholics that drink all of their calories. Has a very pretty yellow color when mixed.

Benzoin: *Great*-smelling liquid that is tacky when dried, helping steri-strips to stay on the skin better. If you sniffed the rubber cement in grade school, you just might like the benzoin solution too.

Benzos: Benzodiazepines. Valium-type medicines that make you feel good and stop seizure activity. They should also be routinely given to the mothers of sick children.

Bicarb: Sodium Bicarbonate. Used to reverse the acid buildup in the blood. Back in the day, it was given to everyone that received CPR. Turns out, it may have killed more than it saved.

CME: Continuing Medical Education or Continuous Memory Eradication.

CPR: Cardio Pulmonary Resuscitation. The fine art of taking a dead person, and through the artful use of drugs, technology, and physical work, keeping them dead, but now dead with broken ribs. Sure, we can "save" some of them, but it is a very small percent for which we are doing any favors.

CVP: Central Venous Pressure. The pressure in the large veins, which contain dark, de-oxygenated blood. If the blood return is bright red, it is in an artery and not a vein.

C1: First cervical vertebrae. The top part of your spine; helps hold your head onto your neck.

Cholecystitis: Gallbladder pain. People with a lot of "F"s: female, fair, fertile, forty, flatulent, and fat, are usually "F"ed.

Clean catch: Easy for most men, but harder for obese women. Hold the skin away from the urine stream so the urine sample can be collected without having it touch any skin on the way out.

Code Blue: Unresponsive person found, or CPR in progress. Named after the patient's skin color, as he hasn't been breathing.

Code Brown: With the standardization of code colors, it actually means something else now, but everyone still uses the original definition of Code Brown—a truly messy crap that must be cleaned up.

Colostomy bag: Bag attached to your abdomen to collect all of the shit that constantly oozes out. The result of some sadistic surgeon who has diverted your bowels away from your ass and out through your belly.

DNR: Do Not Resuscitate. The choice made by some patients or loving family members to accept the fact that the end is near and they don't want to prolong the process by performing CPR or other "heroic" measures.

DOA: Dead on Arrival. When the medics find someone dead enough that they don't even pretend that they can help. Just about the only status patients can receive that guarantees they won't visit the ER later that night.

Enema: Sticking a tube up someone's butt, usually to assist in the evacuation of poop and farts, but sometimes used in trendy clubs in NYC to get a quicker buzz off alcohol that is too bad to drink.

Epi: Epinephrine (adrenaline): When given in high enough doses, you can make a rock start contracting; of course, the rock is still going to stay dead.

Eschmann stylet: Bent guide tube used to assist with intubation when vocal cords can't be seen. It is also the piece of equipment that is moved weekly to a different location, so you can't find it when you need it.

Ewald: Garden-hose-sized tube that is crammed down a patient's throat to instill and then drain large amounts of fluids in an attempt to remove all pill fragments. Can then also be used to instill activated charcoal or a gallon of colon blow to either bind the remaining drugs or push them out the backside before the body can absorb them.

Expectant: Worst group to be triaged into. You are still alive, but you would take too much time and supplies to keep alive, so we are just going to let you die and take care of those we can save. Not used except in mass casualties.

Feculent: Having the qualities of feces. Literally, it means *shitty*.

Fibromyalgia: Name given to chronic pain issues when the primary-care doc is too tired to continue looking for the cause of the pain.

Flagyl: Medicine used to treat many types of infection, including giardia and other causes of diarrhea. Leaves a metallic taste in your mouth and causes you to puke if you mix it with alcohol.

Fnord:

Foley catheter: Tube stuck up the urethra (pee hole) into the bladder to drain urine. Hanging the collection bag to the side of the bed is one good way to keep people from running, as pulling the tube out before deflating the internal balloon can be a bit painful.

Fracture: Broken. A fractured arm means that one of the bones in the arm is broken. An *open* fracture means that the bone popped up through the skin, increasing the risk of infection in the bone. Amazingly, there are many people who, when informed of a fracture, will respond with, "At least it ain't broke."

Gastric lavage: See Ewald.

Gauge: Term used to designate the diameter of needles and shotguns. The smaller the number, the more it is going to hurt.

GI bleed: Bleeding from the gastro-intestinal tract (mouth to ass.) Stool with digested blood in it has an aroma that is nearly diagnostic for a GI bleed. It's not nearly as good smelling as healthy shit.

Glasgow Coma Scale: A scoring system used by EMS to assess survivability and need for advanced airway. Dead people score three out of fifteen points.

Heme: Referring to blood.

Hemorrhoids: Varicose veins of the ass.

Hs and Ts: Pneumonic of "H" and "T" words to help remember the causes of pulseless electrical activity or electro-mechanical dissociation for you old people out there.

Humor: The basis for this book; also, the liquid found in the eye.

HypoXanaxemia: Not having enough Xanax in the bloodstream, leading to anxiety and hyperventilation. Originally called HypoAtivanemia, as Ativan is a better drug, but that just had too many syllables.

Icteric: From the bile produced in the liver. Was also the name of an avant-garde group who put on the exhibit, "Poetry must be made by all / Transform the World."

In/Out collection: Sticking a small(ish) tube up your pee hole to collect a non-contaminated urine specimen for lab. Used on patients that can't provide a clean sample on their own, either due to obesity, menstruation, or loss of consciousness.

Incont: Short for incontinent. One who pees or poops himself. Nursing home patients that are having a Code Brown need to be sent to the ER for evaluation (and cleaning).

Lasix: Brand name of a common diuretic. It makes you pee off the extra fluid floating around your system. Saying you can't take Lasix because it makes you pee is like saying you can't smoke pot because it makes you high and gives you the munchies.

Lung butter: Thick mucus created in the lungs that is both coughed up onto the tongue and then shown to the nurse like a brown, rotting oyster. If the patient is unable to cough up the lung butter, it can be suctioned out, making a hideous slurping noise that almost covers the sounds of the nurses gagging.

Mets: Metastasis. When the cancer is spreading throughout the body instead of staying in one little mass that can be removed. Unlike the baseball team, the Mets, metastasis usually wins.

Midstream: Flushing the urethra out with the first bit of urine, then catching the midstream urine to send to lab. See clean catch.

MRSA: Methicillin-Resistant Staphylococcus Aureus. A common bacterium that has become resistant to certain types of antibiotics. The wounds caused by MRSA will always be blamed on a spider bite, even though methmites are the more common cause.

Mucus plug: Icky OB term. I believe that this is all anyone needs to know about such things.

Narcan: Drug used to reverse the effects of narcotics. Quick way to kill the patient's high, and get thrown up on for your efforts.

Norwegian scabies: Aggressive form of scabies infestation in which the little bugs make cities of bugs and dead skin instead of just little colonies. Believed by most ER staff to be transmitted just by looking at them, or hearing stories of them.

NSAID: Non-Steroidal Anti-Inflammatory Drug, such as Motrin. Works well for muscular, skeletal pain, but amazingly, does not prevent narcotic withdrawals.

Organophosphate: Used in farming, and also in chemical weapons. Causes the signs of SLUDGE.

Osteomyelitis: Infection into the bone. Should be avoided when possible.

Percs: Percocet. Narcotic pain pill. High abuse potential. The drug of choice by patients who remember that they are "allergic" to Vicodin at time of discharge.

Post-void residual: How much pee you have in your bladder right after you urinate.

Precardial thump: Punching someone in the chest to convert a bad rhythm into a good rhythm. Rarely works, but one of the few times you get to punch a patient without getting in trouble—biters being the other time.

Preparation C: Precursor to Preparation H. Term used to make fun of nurses that have hemorrhoids older than most of the medical staff.

Priapism: Constant erection caused by spinal trauma or the sixth grade.

Propofol: Thick, white medicine that puts people into la-la land for a short period of time, affectionately known as *Milk of Amnesia*. Very safe medicine, regardless of what anesthesiologists would lead you to believe.

Pseudo-seizures: Seizure-like activity that is faked, either to get Valium-like medicines or sympathy from friends and family. Can usually be cured with a Foley catheter or some other unpleasant medical procedure.

Pseudocholinesterase: Enzyme used to break down some paralyzing drugs. You aren't moving without it, for a long time.

Psychosocial Dystrophy: A complete inability to control one's emotions, thoughts, actions, and environment. If it ever becomes a billable diagnosis, it will be the number-one diagnosis in the ER. Until then, terms like chronic pain, well-baby check, and pseudo-seizures will remain.

Pulmonary clot: Should have read as *pulmonary embolism,* but that wouldn't fit on the line. A clot that breaks off from somewhere and gets stuck in the lung, causing sudden shortness of breath and a feeling of impending doom. A large enough clot can quickly kill someone. If someone ever says, "I'm going to die," it is a good time to listen, and a better time to report off to a coworker and go to lunch.

Q: Medical shorthand for *every.* Example: Q-2 minutes means that something happens every two minutes.

Quiet: All ER staff knows this word must never be used. You can guarantee that minutes after said word is spoken, all the shit in the world will hit the fan.

RT: Respiratory Therapist. The only people in the known universe that can tolerate the sights, sounds, and smells of lung butter.

Retained enema: Like a regular enema, but a balloon is inflated in the colon to prevent the water from escaping. Helps people hold the fluids in longer to loosen things up a bit. Milk-and-molasses enemas were given this way. They smelled a lot better going in than they did coming out.

Return-flow enema: Lift the enema bucket into the air to fill colon with water, then put it on the ground to siphon everything out. When the fluid is out, it continues to siphon out all of the gas. You can see, hear, and smell the bubbles coming up out of the bucket.

RiG: Rabies immunoglobulin. Given to people who have possibly been exposed to rabies. Not as bad as it used to be, but still not much fun, at least for the patient.

SOB: Short of Breath or Son of a Bitch. Amazingly, some people can be both at the same time.

S1 dermatome: Area of the body innervated from the nerves that come out of the S1 section of the spine. This body area includes the ass sphincter. Bend over, and welcome to Man's Greatest Hospital.

Scroller: A person that has had so many ER visits, that the scroll bar is needed to see them all. Previously called *frequent flyers,* but that implied that we appreciated their business and were happy to give them a discount for their return. The term scroller has more of a negative connotation, meaning someone that abuses the system.

SLUDGE: Salivation, Lacrimation, Urination, Diaphoresis, Gastrointestinal motility, Emesis. Signs of organophosphate toxicity. Everything that can produce or expel fluids is going overtime.

Spankfest: Term of unknown origin. Used when the universe is saying, "You look really busy right now. How about you take a break and bend over for a second?"

Splooge: Not in the dictionary yet, but it is what it sounds like.

STAT: Right now! Stop Talking And Treat.

Steri-strips: Thin pieces of sterile tape to hold wounds together. The only time you get to sniff the benzoin without looking like a freak.

Subcutaneous air: Air that has leaked out of the lungs and is accumulating under the skin. Feels like Rice Krispies.

Succs: Short for succinylcholine chloride. A paralytic drug. Nice to give sedation before you paralyze them, as they remain aware without the sedative, in which case, it Succs to be them.

Suppository: Medicine that can be shoved up your ass. Usually comes in a foil wrapper. It is a sad state of affairs now that we have to tell people to take the foil off before taking the medicine, and that it is not to be swallowed.

Twelve-out-of-ten-pain: Pain is measured on a zero-to-ten scale. People that claim a pain level over ten do not gain extra sympathy from the ER staff. They may be forced to wait a little longer, just for being stupid, especially if they are talking on the cell phone during triage.

Too Drunk To Fish (TDTF): Alcohol has decreased brain function to that of a salad. In less couth places, it is known as *Too Drunk To Fuck*. Occasionally becomes *Too Drunk To Breathe*.

TPA: Clot-busting drug that is approved for certain types of strokes. Needs to be given shortly after symptoms start for any chance of improvement. Sure, it kills some people, but do they really want to live after a big stroke anyway?

Toradol: IV non-narcotic pain medicine. Doesn't play nicely with other drugs in the same tubing, as it tends to form a solid when mixed.

Tramadol: Pain medicine given to people who may need narcotic type pain relief, but who shouldn't be given any of the more addictive opiates. Once people learn that they don't get a high, it will be added to their allergy list.

UTI: Urinary Tract Infection. Unwelcome bacteria between your pee hole and your kidneys. As a general rule, the higher up the tract the bacteria are, the worse you feel.

V-tach: Wide complex rhythm starting in the lower half of the heart. Not a healthy rhythm to be in.

Haiku
STAT!

By Jason Hautala

Upper <u>GI bleed,</u>
How you stink and make a mess.
What is your blood type?

No <u>**BM**</u> for days.
Let us do an <u>enema</u>.
You may feel pressure.

<u>Pulmonary clot</u>.
"I'm going to die," you say.
Odds are, you are right.

<u>CPR</u> Room 5.
Look at the <u>Hs and Ts</u>.
Stop now—<u>DNR</u>.

Mental health eval.
Suicide is what you want.
Then why are you here?

Open leg <u>fracture</u>.
"Go break a leg," means, "Good luck."
Don't be literal.

Overdose on pills.
<u>Gastric lavage</u> with <u>Ewald</u>.
You may gag a bit.

<u>Twelve-out-of-ten pain</u>?
Fractions are misunderstood.
To the waiting room.

<u>UTI</u> symptoms.
Hurts really bad to go pee.
Front-to-back wiping.

Having a baby.
Q-2-minute contractions?
Not in my ER.

Strange rash all over.
Why didn't you tell me that?
Now I itch *a lot.*

Way <u>too drunk to *fish*</u>.
Bets placed on blood alcohol.
584…nice.

<u>MRSA</u> infection.
Blame it on the poor spider.
Methamphetamines.

"No bath for two months?"
"Let's get those dirty socks off."
Inhaled clouds of skin.

<u>CPR</u> Hard. Fast.
"<u>Another One Bites the Dust</u>"
Is the right tempo.

I can't take that med.
It is a bad allergy:
<u>Lasix</u> makes me pee.

Roll her on her side.
What is that <u>feculent</u> smell?
<u>Colostomy bag</u>.

Need lifting help, please.
How can we move this much flesh?
<u>Suppository</u>.

<u>Propofol</u> is great.
Let's pull on that broken arm.
Milk of Amnesia.

Mexican water.
Loose, frothy, explosive stools.
Enjoy the <u>Flagyl</u>.

Did you say *"Quiet"*?
Why would you curse us like that?
Say it again…Die!

Chronic pain issues.
Allergies to all <u>NSAIDs</u>?
Have some <u>Tramadol</u>.

Thirteen-year-old girl.
Never had sex, but pregnant.
It's a miracle.

What day is it now?
Who made this schedule from hell?
More rotating shifts.

Internal bleeding.
Need a couple of IVs.
Go big, or go home.

People are not dogs.
Full life support at all costs.
Wish I were a dog.

Best diagnosis:
<u>Psychosocial Dystrophy</u>.
That sums it up well.

Itching like crazy.
Thick layers of skin and bugs.
<u>Norwegian scabies</u>.

Vomit and feces?
Fine, compared to <u>lung butter</u>.
<u>RTs</u> are crazy.

Heroin is bad.
Methamphetamines are worse.
We need a new drug.

Don't discharge too soon;
Even <u>scrollers</u> can get sick.
Maybe order labs.

<u>Accreditation</u>.
Supposed to help us improve.
At least for a day.

Need <u>Q-*15*</u> checks?
Restrained to the bed with a…
<u>Foley catheter</u>.

Most of brain on bed.
Heart rate and BP still good.
Organ donation.

Code <u>Blue</u> in Room 5.
Code <u>Blue</u> in Room 6, also.
When can I go pee?

No food for five days?
Asparagus-scented pee.
I don't believe you.

Medic line again.
<u>DOA</u> or <u>AMA</u>.
I'm OK with that.

Missed IV again.
Look at those garden hose veins.
I really hate valves.

Is it a full moon?
They say I'm superstitious,
But I believe it.

E-charting is here.
It will capture the charges.
I miss paper charts.

"Please," and "Thank you sir."
"I appreciate your care."
They're from out of town.

Don't hit, kick, spit, bite.
These are simple rules for you.
Break rules, get restrained.

Urine sample sent.
Scan <u>post-void residual</u>.
Too much, need <u>Foley</u>.

<u>Retained enema</u>.
High, hot, and hell of a lot;
Hold it 'til hiccups.

Colon full of gas.
Give <u>return-flow enema</u>.
Enjoy the bubbles.

Drunk driver hit kid.
Nothing we can do for him.
I really hate that.

Extra labs ordered.
Pos. or Neg., no change in plans.
Why order the tests?

Yes, I laugh at pain.
It is not because I'm mean.
No time to cry now.

M.D. on one side.
New nurse on opposite side.
Which way will pus fly?

Seizures get <u>benzos</u>.
Awake with <u>ammonia snap</u>.
Get up from the floor.

Took too many pills.
Drink <u>activated charcoal</u>.
Call housekeeping, please.

Convicted rapist.
I will give excellent care.
Then I hope you hang.

Dominoes of strokes.
<u>TPA</u> in thirty mins,
Or next one, half off.

410 pounds.
<u>Midstream</u>? *Maybe*. <u>Clean catch</u>? *No*.
In/<u>Out</u> collection.

IV <u>Toradol</u>.
Look at the precipitate.
Not compatible.

<u>Hemorrhoids</u> for years.
For well over three decades.
<u>Preparation C</u>.

You need a <u>Foley</u>.
"Look at the length of that tube!"
I hear that a lot.

Remember <u>Bicarb</u>?
Remember high-dose <u>Epi</u>?
Oh, the good old days.

You say you are sick,
Having an emergency.
Get off your cell phone!

98.6
"97 is my norm."
"That is a fever."

Are you still smoking?
<u>Alpha-1 antitrypsin.</u>
It comes in IV.

Don't pull on the cath.
The balloon is inflated.
Look at the prostate.

Post-void, should wash hands.
C-dif, Hep A, E-coli.
Pre-void, *must* wash hands.

You missed the <u>Code Brown</u>.
The stool had maggots inside.
Want some of my rice?

It burns! Make it stop!
WD-40 straw
Not for rectal use.

Afraid of needles,
Body covered in tattoos.
Little sympathy.

Department is full.
Ambulances keep coming.
Laugh or cry, your choice.

"I have some bad news…"
"Your son was shot. He has died."
That call is no fun.

"Thank you for calling,"
"ER, how can I help you?"
Translation: "What now?"

Time for a bed bath.
A lot of folds. Need more wipes.
There is the remote.

Do not hit my staff.
Calm down and stay on the bed.
Police will Tase you.

<u>Adenosine</u> pause.
Sure hope it starts up again.
Seems like a long time.

Your skills saved his life.
Thanks to you, he is alive.
He is suing you.

<u>Precardial thumps</u>.
Evidence shows they don't work;
Sure are fun to do.

Cancer is no sport.
Much different from baseball.
<u>Mets</u> will always win.

What is that rhythm?
<u>Aberrancy</u> or <u>V-tach</u>?
Who cares? No pulse, shock.

No more than two beers.
Never fewer than two dudes.
Ever hear the truth?

Friday the Thirteenth
Was bad for The Knights Templar.
Bad for ER too.

Don't be overweight.
Volume of <u>RiG</u> is weight based.
Five shots for you now.

Mad about long wait.
Breathing fine, just really mad.
Old school <u>SOB</u>.

You are female, fair,
Fertile, forty, flatulent.
<u>Cholecystitis</u>.

<u>Mucus plug</u> on floor.
<u>Splooge</u> of fluid in my shoe.
You must be pregnant.

High pain tolerance.
It is bad if I am here.
Ouch...BP cuff tight.

Heroin junkie,
Please do not use your last vein.
It's for me someday.

Belly-button lint?
Rhino horn and thick, brown paste.
No way is that lint!

Movement felt in ear.
Cockroaches can't move backwards.
Bugs can be icky.

What the hell is that?
Lab hates my gifts of fluids.
Slight odor to some.

You have to stand up.
No, I won't let you fall down—
Too much paperwork.

No rattlesnakes here,
Yet you managed to get bit?
Alcohol involved.

Trampolines are fun.
Broken arms and head trauma.
Job security.

<u>Benzoin</u> smells quite nice.
It helps <u>steri-strips</u> stay on.
I like it too much.

Suicide attempt.
Think how that would hurt your friends.
Selfish little prick.

Snipers have motto:
"One shot, one kill." They stole it.
New grads use the same.

If there is a fire,
Evacuate all patients,
Except those that spit.

Does it have a name?
The loose, dry skin on elbow.
That is your *wenis.*

Can't walk to restroom.
Up to the bedside commode.
Fecal position.

Waiting-room drama.
The squeaky wheel gets the grease,
Or it is replaced.

Coded twice this month.
Sometimes winning is losing.
Best to die healthy.

You should cut out fat.
No added salt or sugar.
Don't do as I do.

Quantity makes up
What we lack in quality.
Can't have both of them.

Projectile vomit.
You used the last vomit bag.
Restock them, or clean.

Sedated patient.
M.D. with very bad gas.
Who is getting blamed?

It is discharge time.
Even though you are homeless,
You just can't stay here.

He is going home?
He shot himself in the gut.
Signed no-harm contract.

I said, "Little prick."
No, you aren't getting a shot.
<u>Foley catheter</u>.

"My daughter hits me."
"I don't want to go back there."
I'll call <u>APS</u>.

"Why are you so wet?"
Drunken meth-head was raging,
Threw the urinal.

Suture removal.
Damn those facial-plastics docs.
Time for bifocals.

Arterial bleed.
First to stick finger in hole.
Stuck there 'til OR.

How did this happen?
Cigarette burns to son's back.
Lucky I'm not armed.

Screaming, painful death.
"Was he in pain when he died?"
"No, just fell asleep."

Women love cool scars.
Mine are all emotional;
Yours will be sexy.

Diagnostic test.
Therapeutic procedure.
Punitive twelve <u>gauge</u>.

I used to hate death.
"I can keep people alive."
Some wouldn't want this.

Four in hallway beds.
Twenty in the waiting room.
It is a <u>spankfest</u>.

I have to go pee.
Another ambulance here.
Where is my leg bag?

Vomit on ceiling.
Volume scores only a three;
Placement gets a nine.

Do not speak that name.
If he shows up here today,
I will kill you…twice.

Stop talking to me.
Your voice gives me a migraine.
Please bring Demerol.

He is very nice.
He did not hit or bite me.
Expectations low.

Jason Hautala

Worst day of their lives.
Often the very last day,
But I made some laugh.

What is that alarm?
Something bad going on here.
Fries done? Or guy dead?

Beauty is skin deep.
<u>Osteomyelitis</u>,
That is to the bone.

Give a compliment:
"I love your beautiful veins."
Pickup-line failure.

ER folks cope well.
Bury it deep down in soul.
With luck, it won't stain.

Tall boy with chest pain.
Feel <u>subcutaneous air</u>
Snap, crackle, and pop.

Ass foreign body.
Sometimes you just have to ask,
"How did that get there?"

Dyspnea, tingles.
<u>HypoXanaxemia</u>,
That is what you have.

Wailing, widowed wife.
Tissues, kind words, pat on back.
Couldn't help either.

Personal info…
It will be used against you.
Love my coworkers.

Dr. H is here.
He is such a shit magnet.
Pain must be ferrous.

Medic phone report:
Acute chest pain. <u>AMA</u>?
Some patients are dumb.

Red or green freeze-pop?
Choices were fun as a kid.
Red stool or brown pus?

Not just alcohol;
He is mad as a hatter.
Must be tequila.

Brain already full.
Mandatory <u>CME</u>.
Purge more memories.

Please say, "Chronic pain."
Don't say, "<u>Fibromyalgia</u>."
We can treat the pain.

Want pregnancy test?
Go to free clinic or store.
Tax money at work.

Mommy is in pain.
Last ER wouldn't give <u>Percs</u>.
Are you bastards here?

No pill fragments found.
Looks like he ate beans and rice.
What's for lunch today?

Face and airway burns.
Nasal cannula caught fire.
Smoking *can* kill you.

Need to take pants off.
You should have listened to Mom.
Put on clean undies.

MVA, three dead.
Drunk driver…no injuries.
Children should drink more.

Any prior care?
Other hospital armband.
Take it off next time.

Please God, let me die.
It is too much; can't go on.
Shift only half done.

Need script for Motrin.
Can't afford that wrist-pain med.
Trade you for your smokes.

Meth-head with a knife.
Someone call security.
Need a male nurse...<u>STAT</u>.

Only one patient,
Brought by two ambulances.
Bad day for someone.

Is health care a right?
ER for primary care?
Another way please.

Days spent in ER
Holding patients for rule-outs.
Hospital still there?

You have orifice.
We have a tube that will fit.
We'll even make some.

When you really care,
Giving all you have to give
Just isn't enough.

Hospitality…
There is nothing else as great,
But we can't bill it.

That's a lot of blood.
Hope this tampon fits in there.
Nasal bleeds are gross.

Knee dislocation.
<u>Avascular necrosis</u>.
Should have checked blood flow.

Quit job of eight years.
Replacement nurse got killed there.
Feel a bit guilty.

Busload of patients.
Sixty arrive at one time.
Poor charting that night.

If I were not me,
What would my opinion be
Of humanity?

Meet on the level.
There's hope for the widow's son.
It's why I am here.

Delayed or urgent.
Triage is normally fun.
<u>Expectant</u>…tough call.

<u>Glasgow Coma Scale</u>.
Even dead people get three.
I feel like a two.

Too many visits.
Scroll bar needed to see them.
You are a "<u>scroller</u>."

Wires and tubing.
What a tangled mess they make.
Must fight entropy.

Let the *humor* out.
When it comes to your eyeball,
Keep the <u>humor</u> in.

Play with fire nude?
Watch out for that 1%.
(4% for me.)

Happy to see me?
No. <u>C1</u> dislocation.
That's <u>priapism</u>.

Abdomen CT.
He weighs 200 kilos.
Need a bigger hole.

Three-hundred pound man.
Gown put on with slit to front.
Don't need to see that.

Ultrasound shows vein.
Heroin can't reach this one.
Enjoy the <u>Narcan</u>.

Drug screen positive.
He said he didn't do drugs.
Machine must be wrong.

Serious road rash.
Scrub, scrub, scrub, scrub, scrub, scrub, scrub,
Scrub, scrub, scrub, scrub, scrub.

All IVs labeled.
Use this for <u>banana bag</u>.
Mountain Dew logo.

Coding Santa Claus.
Went down at the shopping mall.
He's not immortal.

Nursing home report:
"Bone sticking out through the skin."
No wound, just <u>incont</u>.

Helping people die,
<u>Enemas</u>, and <u>Foley caths</u>:
Things I've been thanked for.

Ask the doctor first,
"Want them too long? Or too short?"
Cutting suture thread.

Overhead <u>STAT</u> call.
ER needs assistance…Now!
No coffee creamer.

You made a mistake?
"Didn't chart, didn't do it."
Sometimes less is more.

Like well-oiled machine,
Smoothest <u>Code Blue</u> we have had.
Figures...he still died.

Soldiers in ER,
Thank you for your brave service.
How can we serve you?

Way too many meds.
Thank you for having a list.
Next time, bring *your* list.

Time of death: right now.
Turn off the vent and IVs.
Shit, he has a pulse.

Sure, we can crack chest.
Although, if he's not dead yet,
He will be shortly.

Huge tongue and no neck.
Add anterior airway.
Find <u>Eschmann stylet</u>.

Deficient in this:
<u>Pseudocholinesterase</u>.
<u>Succs</u> might work too long.

Won't float to ER?
Why is everyone afraid?
Are we asocial?

Be rich, make patent.
Works on Earth, what about space?
Chest tube, water seal.

Wreck a quad, be one.
All good things must come to end;
Bad things might not end.

Nature or nurture?
Inherit diarrhea;
It runs in your genes.

He has signs of <u>SLUDGE</u>.
<u>Organophosphate</u> toxic.
Need more <u>Atropine</u>.

Hyperthermic death.
Not heat, but humanity.
Cocaine overdose.

Work in ER long,
It will twist your perception.
Not saying it's good.

Life in the ER
Patients come, and patients go.
More come than go, though.

Eye chemical burn.
Dilution for pollution.
Works for oil spills too.

You have been discharged.
Won't leave without narcotics?
Cops will escort you.

Dark pee in cath bag.
Dehydrated, white bubbles.
<u>Icteric</u>, brown froth.

Check the <u>CVP</u>.
One twenty over eighty.
Thought the blood was bright.

BA 500.
I would pay good money for
Alcohol <u>Narcan</u>.

"Little poke and burn."
Digital blocks seem to hurt.
Reason for blade guard.

Wife down in OB.
"Since I'm here, get this looked at."
Sorry for your kid.

Stop cutting yourself.
At least make pretty designs.
Scars should tell stories.

Stick tongue out to think.
Need to break this habit soon.
<u>Enema</u> splash...ick.

Fluff your pillow, Sir?
Wipe your ass for you, Madam?
For this I had school.

Why do you work here?
Fight or flight, or stay and play?
Both have their moments.

Lost a body part.
Maybe we can sew it on?
Sorry, dog ate it.

Abrasions with tar.
Road tar is hard to get out.
Mayonnaise is key.

<u>Heme</u>-positive stool.
Checking <u>S1 dermatome</u>.
Rip in glove finger.

12413983R00080

Made in the USA
Lexington, KY
08 December 2011